KATHERINE DEARLOVE   LORI JOY SMITH

my CANADA

AN ILLUSTRATED ATLAS

OWLKIDS BOOKS

Oh, Canada

Canadian Flag

National Symbols

beaver

Canadian horse

lacrosse
(national summer sport)

hockey
(national winter sport)

When you think of Canada, what comes to mind? Maybe you think of the maple leaf, a beaver, or hockey—they're our national symbols, after all. Or maybe you picture our country's snowy mountains, endless forests, or busy cities. What about maple syrup? Lacrosse? Or your very own neighbourhood? The list could go on and on because Canada is all these things and so much more!

Canada has been a country since 1867. We think its name came from the Huron-Iroquois word for "village." But Canada is more than just a village today. It's the world's second biggest country, stretching all the way from British Columbia in the west to Newfoundland and Labrador in the east, and from the United States in the south to the Arctic in the north.

My Canada takes you across our amazing country, stopping in each province and territory. The museums and monuments, wildlife and waterways, sights and shorelines all tell a story about Canada and the many different people, places, and landscapes you'll find here. Are you ready to explore Canada from coast to coast to coast? Let's get going!

Legend

 Canada's Capital City

 Provincial/ Territorial Capital City

 City

 National Park

Did you know that Canada has

3 territories and 10 provinces;

the world's **longest coastline;**

more lakes than any other country;

the world's **longest international border;**

 more than **36 million people** living mostly in cities along our southern border;

2 official **languages,** French and English;

More than **60 Aboriginal languages;**

speakers of more than **200 world languages;**

 and **more than half** of the **world's polar bears?**

Arctic
Ocean

United
States

Yukon

Northwest
Territories

Nunavut

Pacific
Ocean

★
WHITEHORSE

★
YELLOWKNIFE

British
Columbia

Alberta

Manitoba

Saskatchewan

N

W ● E

S

★
EDMONTON

★
VICTORIA

★
REGINA

★
WINNIPEG

United States

Greenland

Canada

Baffin Bay

IQALUIT ★

Newfoundland
and Labrador

Labrador
Sea

Hudson
Bay

St. JOHN'S ★

Prince Edward
Island

Quebec

CHARLOTTETOWN ★

Nova Scotia

Ontario

HALIFAX ★

FREDERICTON ★

New Brunswick

QUEBEC CITY ★

Lake
Superior

OTTAWA ★

Lake
Huron

Lake Ontario

Atlantic
Ocean

TORONTO ★

Lake
Michigan

Lake Erie

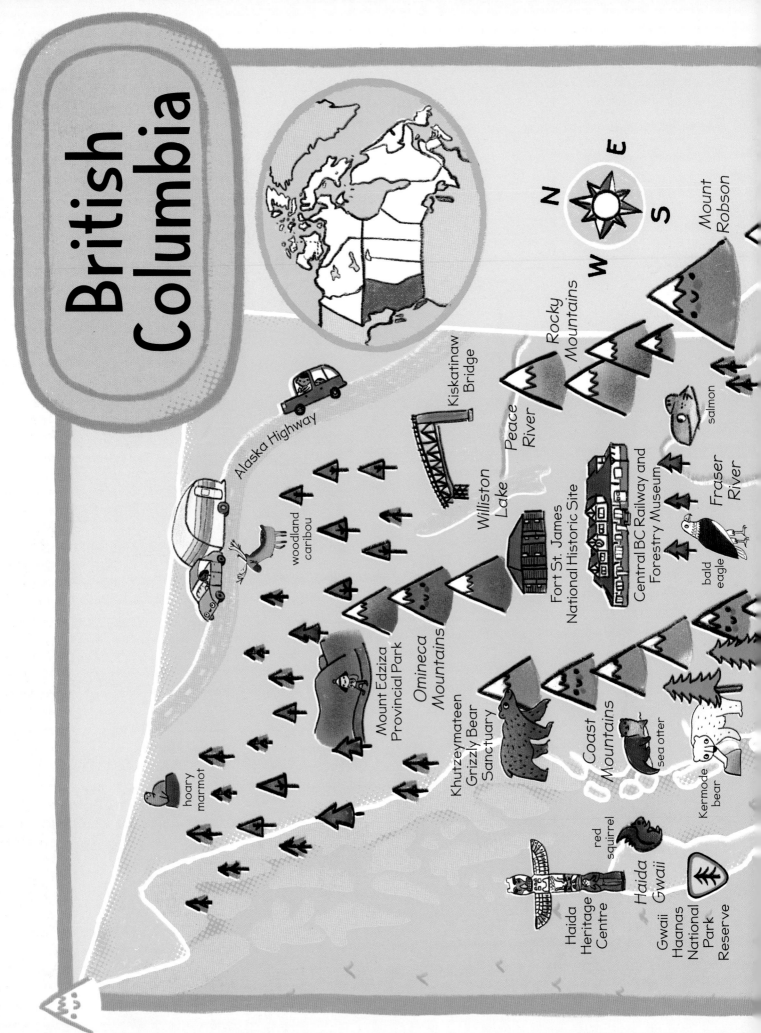

British Columbia

Queen Charlotte Sound

Barkerville Historic Town

Kinbasket Lake

white-tailed deer

Radium Hot Springs

Columbia River

Cape Scott Provincial Park

cougar

Whistler Mountain

Ogopogo

Okanagan Valley

boreal toad

orca whales

Pacific green turtle

Pacific Ocean

Vancouver Island

VANCOUVER

VICTORIA

Provincial Flag

Provincial Symbols

western red cedar

Pacific dogwood

Steller's jay

Sea to Sky Gondola

Fraser River

Stanley Park

Vancouver Chinatown

Della Falls

Nanaimo bar

The Butchart Gardens

Peace Arch

VANCOUVER

VICTORIA

Hanging Garden Tree

Emily Carr House

Salish Sea

Vancouver Island

Alberta

Provincial Flag

Provincial Symbols

great horned owl

wild rose

lodgepole pine

moose

Slave River

Lake Athabasca

Wood Buffalo National Park

wood bison

bull trout

boreal chorus frog

Athabasca oil sands

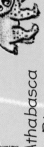
lynx

Athabasca River

Peace River

Peace River Bridge

black bear

grey wolf

Lesser Slave Lake

Dunvegan Provincial Park

grouse

golden eagle

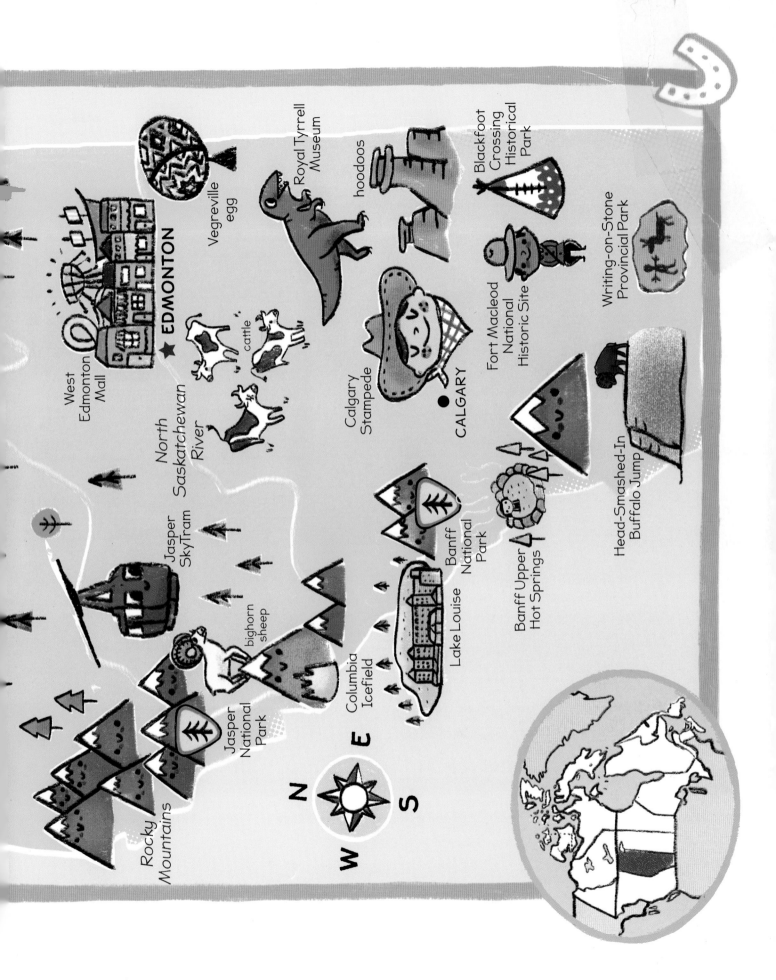

West Edmonton Mall

Vegreville egg

★ EDMONTON

cattle

North Saskatchewan River

Royal Tyrrell Museum

hoodoos

Blackfoot Crossing Historical Park

Calgary Stampede

CALGARY

Fort Macleod National Historic Site

Writing-on-Stone Provincial Park

Jasper SkyTram

bighorn sheep

Jasper National Park

Columbia Icefield

Lake Louise

Banff National Park

Banff Upper Hot Springs

Head-Smashed-In Buffalo Jump

Rocky Mountains

N
W · E
S

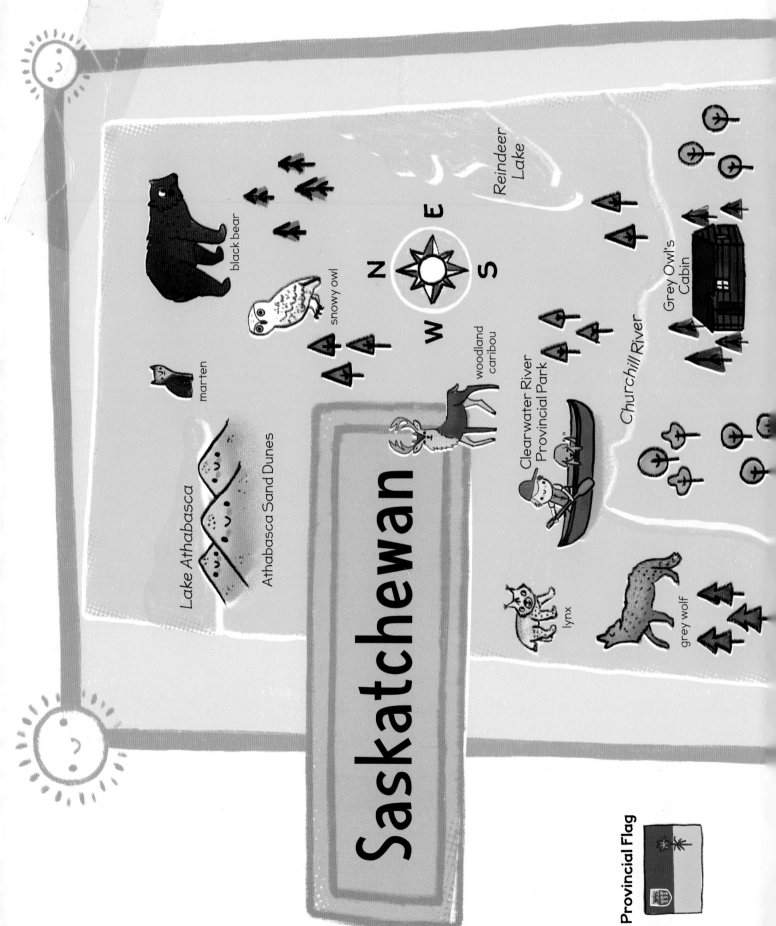

Saskatchewan

black bear

snowy owl

marten

Lake Athabasca

Athabasca Sand Dunes

Reindeer Lake

N
W E
S

woodland caribou

Clearwater River Provincial Park

Churchill River

Grey Owl's Cabin

lynx

grey wolf

Provincial Flag

Provincial Symbols

sharp-tailed grouse

western red lily

white birch

Saskatoon berries

Saskatchewan River

lentils

Batoche National Historic Site

chickpeas

Little Manitou Lake

Qu'Appelle Valley

Lgjord Hutterite Colony

REGINA

RCMP Heritage Centre

sunshine capital of Canada

red fox

Diefenbaker House

North Saskatchewan River

white-tailed jackrabbits

Fort Carlton Provincial Park

mustard

Wanuskewin Heritage Park

SASKATOON

South Saskatchewan River

Tunnels of Moose Jaw

Cypress Hills

prairie rattlesnake

Grasslands National Park

Big Muddy Badlands

Manitoba

Provincial Flag

Provincial Symbols

 great grey owl

 prairie crocus

 white spruce

 beluga whale

Hudson Bay

 snow goose

N E
W S

Wapusk National Park

 polar bears

walleye

 lynx

Prince of Wales Fort

 willow ptarmigan

 Sand Lakes Provincial Park

Nelson River

moose

river otter

Arctic hare

grey wolf

barren-ground caribou

Churchill River

Reindeer Lake

grey jay

black bear

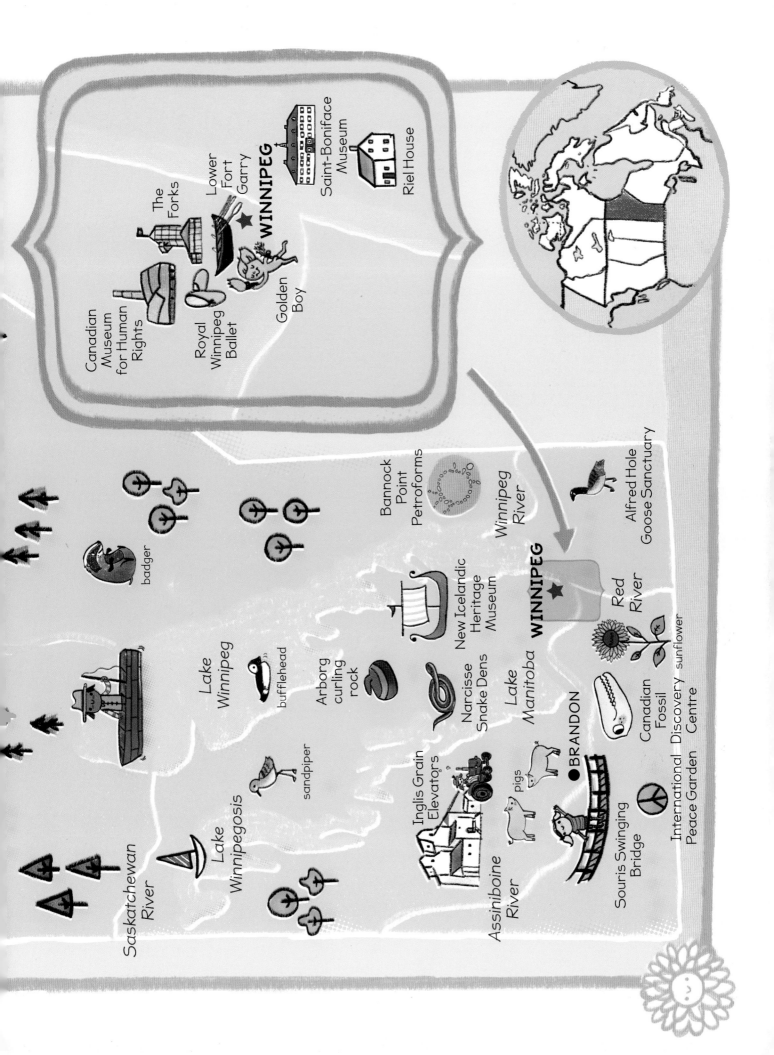

The Forks

Canadian Museum for Human Rights

Lower Fort Garry

Royal Winnipeg Ballet

Saint-Boniface Museum

WINNIPEG

Golden Boy

Riel House

Saskatchewan River

badger

Lake Winnipeg

bufflehead

Lake Winnipegosis

sandpiper

Arborg curling rock

Bannock Point Petroforms

Winnipeg River

New Icelandic Heritage Museum

Narcisse Snake Dens

Lake Manitoba

WINNIPEG

Alfred Hole Goose Sanctuary

Red River

Inglis Grain Elevators

pigs

●BRANDON

Assiniboine River

Souris Swinging Bridge

Canadian Fossil

International Peace Garden

Discovery Centre

sunflower

Hudson Bay

woodland caribou

Polar Bear Provincial Park

halibut

James Bay

beluga whale

marten

walrus

seal

eastern garter snake

moose

Wabakimi Provincial Park

black bear

Moonbeam Flying Saucer

beaver

skunk

Lake Nipigon

shadfly

raccoon

Mather-Walls House

Lake of the Woods Museum

Terry Fox monument

Sleeping Giant Provincial Park

Wawa Goose

fox

Fort William Historical Park

THUNDER BAY

Lake Superior

Canadian Bushplane Heritage Centre

Killarney Provincial Park

Lake Michigan

N

E

W

S

Sainte-Marie among the Hurons

Lake Huron

CN Tower

Hockey Hall of Fame

Lake Ontario

pigeon

★ **TORONTO**

Mennonite Story Visitor Centre

Royal Ontario Museum

Oil Museum of Canada

Uncle Tom's Cabin Historic Site

Oktoberfest

Niagara Falls

Point Pelee National Park

Lake Erie

blue jay

Ottawa River

Parliament Hill

★ **OTTAWA**

Big Nickel

Science North

Algonquin Provincial Park

Upper Canada Village

St. Lawrence River

Georgian Bay

Group of Seven Outdoor Gallery

Canadian Canoe Museum

Lake Huron

Lake Ontario

TORONTO ★

Lake Erie

Provincial Flag

Provincial Symbols

common loon

white trillium

eastern white pine

Ontario

Quebec

sperm whale

humpback whale

Labrador Sea

N E S W

Hudson Strait

Ungava Bay

Kuururjuaq National Park

black bear

Kuujjuaq

caribou

peregrine falcon

northern pike

snowshoe hare

muskox

Pingualuit Crater

polar bears

Hudson Bay

Daniel Weetaluktuk Memorial Museum

Arctic fox

marten

moose

grey wolf

Robert-Bourassa Generating Station

James Bay

beluga whale

Atlantic salmon

Gulf of St. Lawrence

little brown bat

Mingan Archipelago National Park Reserve

St. Lawrence River

Anticosti Island

Pierced Rock

Magdalen Islands

Miguasha National Park

Manicouagan Crater

Daniel-Johnson Dam

Appalachian Mountains

Pointe-au-Père Maritime Historical Site

Lake Mistassini

Saguenay Fjord

Aanischaaukamikw Cree Cultural Institute

Lake Saint-Jean

Quebec Winter Carnival

QUEBEC CITY

Citadelle of Quebec

maple syrup

robin

bumblebee

Olympic Stadium

Biosphere

MONTREAL

Mont-Tremblant

Ottawa River

Canadian Museum of History

Provincial Symbols

snowy owl

blue flag iris

yellow birch

Provincial Flag

Appalachian
Mountains

black
bear

Sugarloaf
Provincial Park

Chaleur
Bay

Mount Carleton

Acadian
Historical
Village

fiddlehead

Grand
Falls

Maritime
garter snake

Kouchibouguac
National Park

groundhog

dragonfly

Miramichi
River

white-tailed
deer

muskrat

Hartland
Bridge

Historic
Garrison
District

fox

Grand Lake

FREDERICTON

Fundy
National
Park

The
Chocolate
Museum

raccoon

coyote

lupine

Saint
John River

Swallowtail
Lightstation

Grand
Manan
Island

St. Andrews
Blockhouse

Carleton
Martello
Tower

Reversing
Rapids

Bay of Fundy
Mudflats

Bay of
Fundy

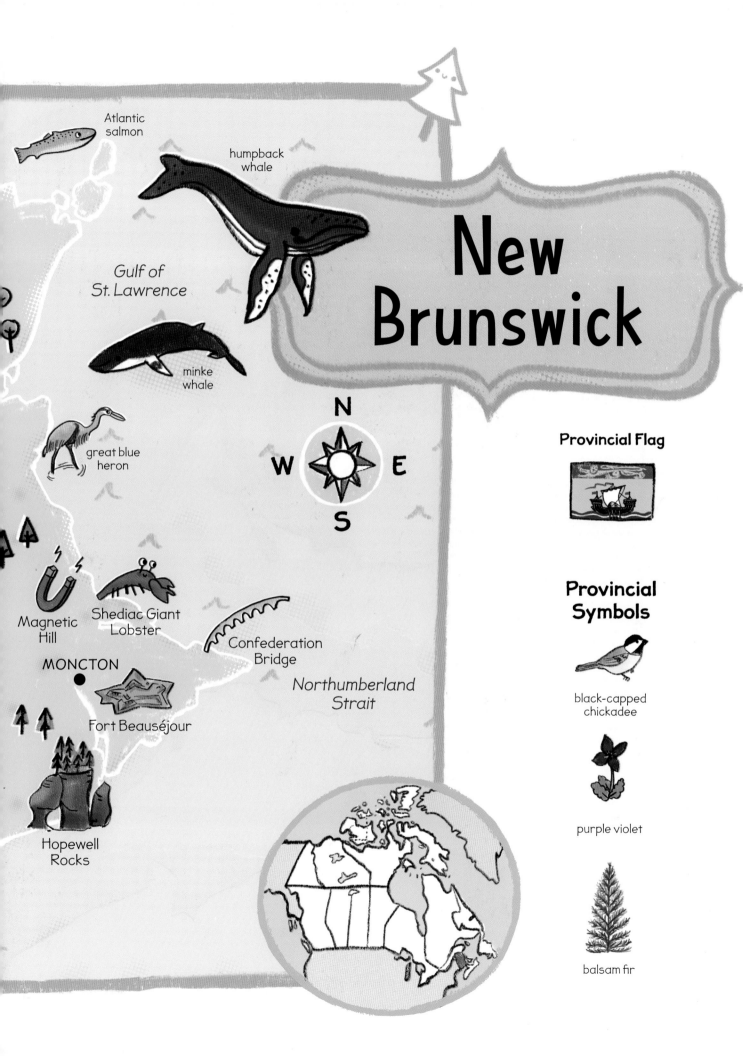

New Brunswick

Atlantic salmon

humpback whale

Gulf of St. Lawrence

minke whale

great blue heron

Magnetic Hill

Shediac Giant Lobster

MONCTON

Fort Beauséjour

Confederation Bridge

Northumberland Strait

Hopewell Rocks

Provincial Flag

Provincial Symbols

black-capped chickadee

purple violet

balsam fir

Nova Scotia

Joggins Fossil Cliffs

Northumberland Strait

oyster

eastern painted turtle

green frog

Fundy Geological Museum

Grand-Pré National Historic Site

blueberries

Cape Split

Bay of Fundy

harbour porpoise

Annapolis Valley

Halifax Public Gardens

Citadel Hill

Lawrencetown Beach

Fort Anne National Historic Site

Peggy's Point Lighthouse

Pier 21

Kejimkujik National Park

red fox

Lake Rossignol

Old Town Lunenburg

HALIFAX

Port-Royal National Historic Site

HMCS Sackville

eastern chipmunk

trout

Black Loyalist Heritage Centre

Bluenose II

Cabot
Trail

Cape Breton
Highlands
National Park

Marconi
National
Historic
Site

SYDNEY

Alexander Graham Bell
National Historic Site

bobcat

Fortress of
Louisbourg

lobster

beaver

Bras d'Or
Lake

Cape Breton
Island

Antigonish
Highland
Games

St. Peters Canal
National Historic Site

Nova Scotia Duck
Tolling Retriever

woodpecker

Atlantic
Ocean

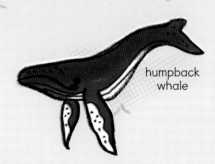

humpback
whale

Sable Island
horse

Sable
Island

Provincial Flag

Provincial Symbols

osprey

mayflower

red spruce

North Cape Wind Energy Interpretive Centre

Gulf of St. Lawrence

snowshoe hare

dolphin

purple finch

The Canadian Potato Museum

leatherback sea turtle

Confederation Trail

West Point Lighthouse

Green Park Shipbuilding Museum

Acadian Museum

Malpeque oyster

halibut

porcupine

Brackley Beach

PEI National Park

Kensington Haunted Mansion

Green Gables Heritage Place

Dalvay-by-the-Sea

The Bottle Houses

The College of Piping

SUMMERSIDE

PEI 1864 Sculpture

1864

CHARLOTTETOWN ★

lupine

Beaconsfield Historic House

Confederation Bridge

Port-la-Joye—Fort Amherst

ring-necked duck

humpback whale

N
W E
S

Prince Edward Island

East Point
Lighthouse

Elmira Railway
Museum

lobster

Confederation
Trail

Basin Head
Singing Sands
Beach

Basin Head
Fisheries
Museum

Orwell Corner
Historic Village

harbour
seal

eastern
coyote

cardinal

red-bellied
snake

Northumberland Strait

Provincial Flag

Provincial Symbols

blue jay

lady's slipper

red oak

Newfoundland and Labrador

Provincial Symbols

 Atlantic puffin

 pitcher plant

 black spruce

Provincial Flag

 humpback whale

N
W · E
S

Labrador Sea

 Arctic char

harbour seals

Illusuak Cultural Centre

Hopedale Mission National Historic Site

Torngat Mountains National Park

muskox

Mount Caubvick

 polar bear

caribou

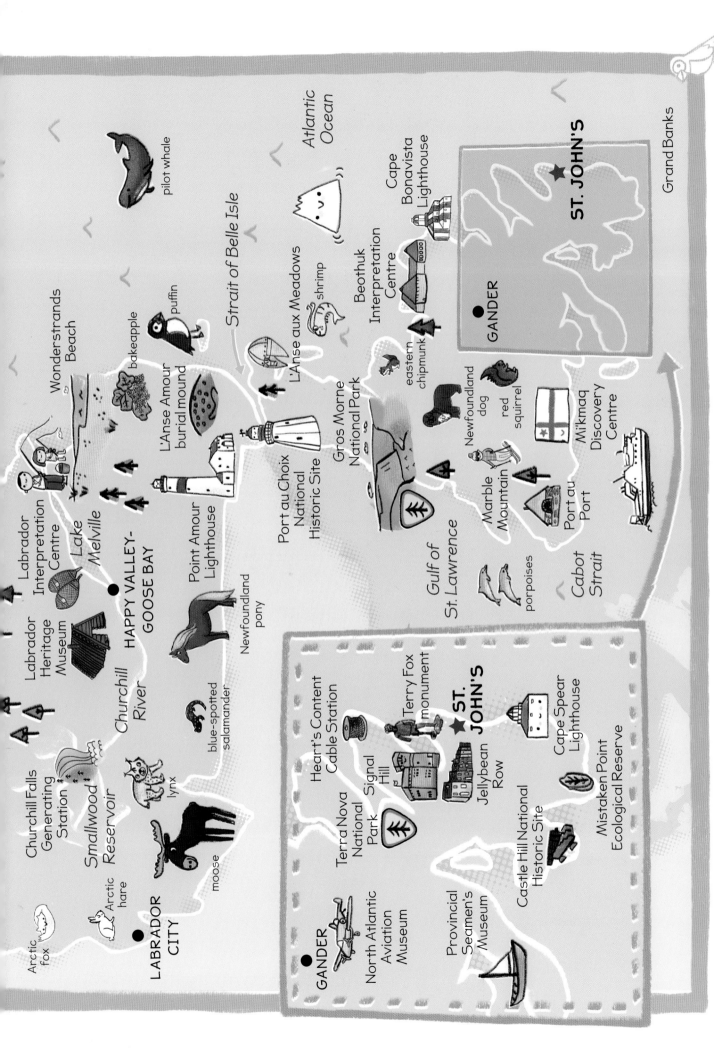

Atlantic Ocean

pilot whale

Strait of Belle Isle

L'Anse aux Meadows

shrimp

Beothuk Interpretation Centre

Cape Bonavista Lighthouse

Grand Banks

ST. JOHN'S

GANDER

eastern chipmunk

Newfoundland dog

red squirrel

Mi'kmaq Discovery Centre

Port au Port

Marble Mountain

Cabot Strait

porpoises

Gulf of St. Lawrence

Gros Morne National Park

Port au Choix National Historic Site

L'Anse Amour burial mound

Point Amour Lighthouse

Newfoundland pony

bakeapple

puffin

Wonderstrands Beach

Labrador Interpretation Centre

Lake Melville

HAPPY VALLEY-GOOSE BAY

Churchill River

Labrador Heritage Museum

Churchill Falls Generating Station

Smallwood Reservoir

lynx

blue-spotted salamander

moose

Arctic hare

Arctic fox

LABRADOR CITY

GANDER

North Atlantic Aviation Museum

Provincial Seamen's Museum

Terra Nova National Park

Signal Hill

Heart's Content Cable Station

Terry Fox monument

ST. JOHN'S

Jellybean Row

Castle Hill National Historic Site

Cape Spear Lighthouse

Mistaken Point Ecological Reserve

Yukon

N W E S

Arctic Circle

Beaufort Sea

Vuntut National Park

Ivvavik National Park

woodland caribou

lemming

snowshoe hare

John Tizya Centre

fox

Arctic grayling

Palace Grand Theatre

●DAWSON

Yukon Quest

peregrine falcon

lynx

Dempster Highway

Keno City Mining Museum

Binet House

Klondike Goldfields

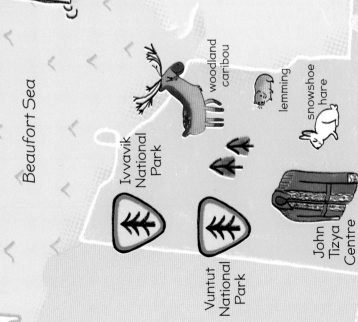

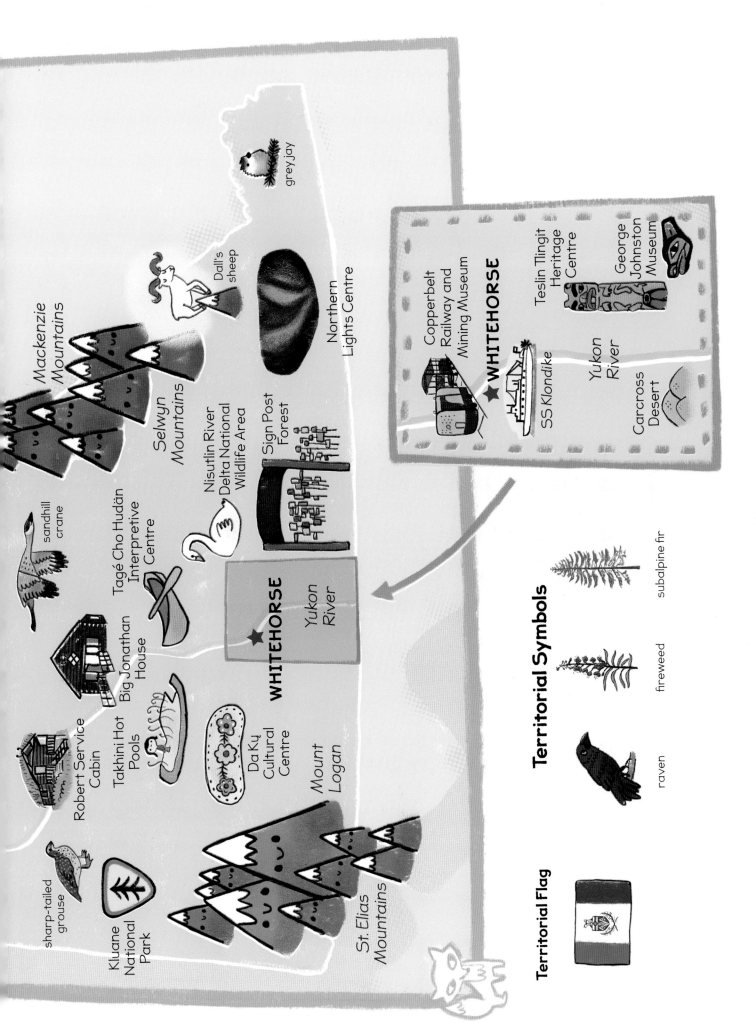

grey jay

Mackenzie
Mountains

Dall's
sheep

Selwyn
Mountains

Northern
Lights Centre

Nisutlin River
Delta National
Wildlife Area

Sign Post
Forest

sandhill
crane

Tagé Cho Hudän
Interpretive
Centre

Robert Service
Cabin

Big Jonathan
House

Takhini Hot
Pools

Da Kų
Cultural
Centre

WHITEHORSE

Yukon
River

sharp-tailed
grouse

Kluane
National
Park

Mount
Logan

St. Elias
Mountains

Copperbelt
Railway and
Mining Museum

Teslin Tlingit
Heritage
Centre

George
Johnston
Museum

WHITEHORSE

SS Klondike

Yukon
River

Carcross
Desert

Territorial Symbols

raven

fireweed

subalpine fir

Territorial Flag

Northwest Territories

Arctic Ocean

Prince Patrick Island

Melville Island

Arctic hare

beluga whale

polar bears

Victoria Island

Arctic fox

Holman Golf Course

Aulavik National Park

lesser snow goose

Banks Island

muskox

Beaufort Sea

Tuktut Nogait National Park

Acasta Gneiss

The Smoking Hills

moose

Our Lady of Victory Church

●INUVIK

Arctic cotton grass

bald eagle

pingos

Mackenzie River

Dempster Highway

Dall's sheep

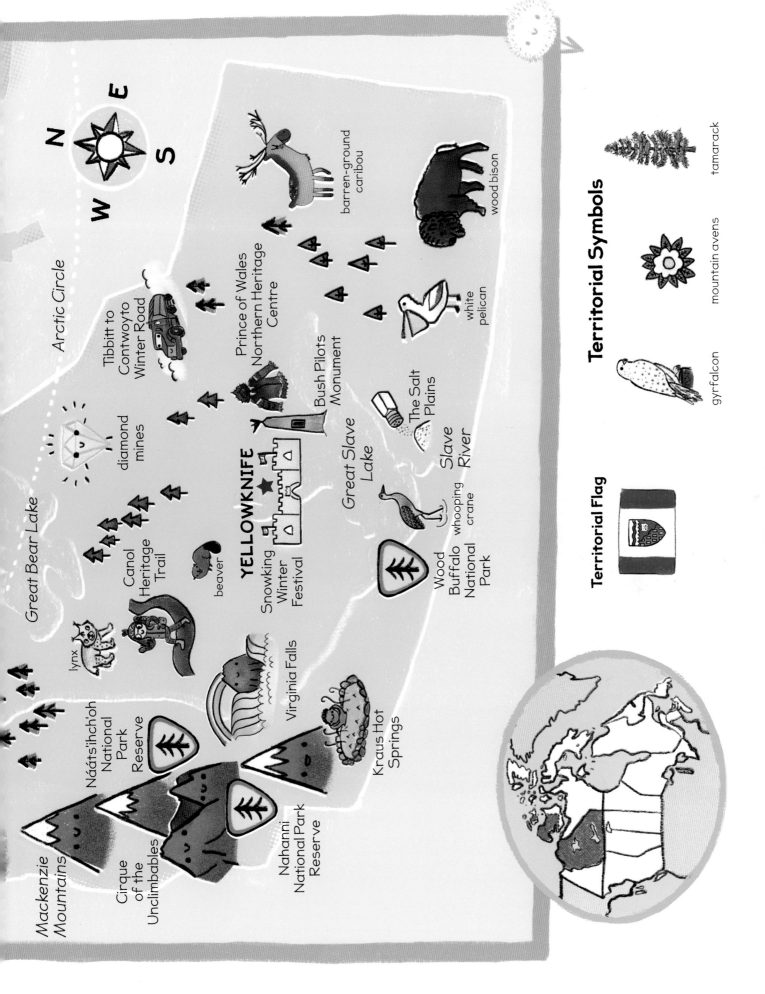

Mackenzie Mountains

Cirque of the Unclimbables

Náàts'ihch'oh National Park Reserve

Nahanni National Park Reserve

Kraus Hot Springs

Virginia Falls

lynx

beaver

Great Bear Lake

Canol Heritage Trail

diamond mines

Arctic Circle

Tibbitt to Contwoyto Winter Road

YELLOWKNIFE

Snowking Winter Festival

Prince of Wales Northern Heritage Centre

Bush Pilots Monument

Great Slave Lake

The Salt Plains

Slave River

whooping crane

Wood Buffalo National Park

barren-ground caribou

wood bison

white pelican

N W E S

Territorial Flag

Territorial Symbols

gyrfalcon   mountain avens   tamarack

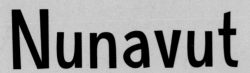

Nunavut

bowhead
whale

*Arctic
Ocean*

Arctic
char

Territorial Flag

Territorial Symbols

rock ptarmigan

purple saxifrage

Canadian
Inuit dog

*Victoria
Island*

walrus

*Arctic
Circle*

barren-ground
caribou

Arctic
woolly bear
caterpillar

Alert

Lake Hazen

muskox

Quttinirpaaq National Park

Ellesmere Island

gyrfalcon

ringed seal

Sirmilik National Park

narwhal

Baffin Bay

Thor Peak

Arctic Circle

Arctic fox

Nattinnak Centre

lichen

Baffin Island

Auyuittuq National Park

Uqqurmiut Centre for Arts and Crafts

snowy owl

Dewey Soper Migratory Bird Sanctuary

Legislative Assembly of Nunavut

northern lights

moose

wolverine

HMS *Erebus* shipwreck

Ukkusiksalik National Park

Arctic wolf

Cape Dorset Inuit Art Gallery

IQALUIT ★

Road to Nowhere

St. Jude's Cathedral

Arctic cotton grass

Fall Caribou Crossing National Historic Site

snowshoe hare

inuksuk

● **RANKIN INLET**

beluga whale

Hudson Bay

polar bear

To Randy, Olivia, and Nate
~KD

For Paul
~LJS

Creating a book about our massive, amazing country required a team effort, and I'd like to thank everyone at Owlkids for their hard work and insightful suggestions: Karen B., Debbie, Judy, and Sarah. Also Lori Joy Smith, whose charming illustrations brought warmth and whimsy to the maps, and Diane Robertson, whose excellent design work pulled it all together. And special thanks to Maria Birmingham for her thoughtful editing, late-night fact-checking, and keen eye for detail. It's been a great trip!

~Katherine Dearlove

Text © 2017 Katherine Dearlove
Illustrations © 2017 Lori Joy Smith

Owlkids Books acknowledges the financial support of the Canada Council for the Arts, the Ontario Arts Council, the Government of Canada through the Canada Book Fund (CBF) and the Government of Ontario through the Ontario Media Development Corporation's Book Initiative for our publishing activities.

Published in Canada by
Owlkids Books Inc.
10 Lower Spadina Avenue
Toronto, ON M5V 2Z2

Published in the United States by
Owlkids Books Inc.
1700 Fourth Street
Berkeley, CA 94710

Library and Archives Canada Cataloguing in Publication

Dearlove, Katherine, author

My Canada : an illustrated atlas / written by Katherine Dearlove; illustrated by Lori Joy Smith.

ISBN 978-1-77147-264-7 (hardback)--ISBN 978-1-77147-302-6 (pbk.)

1. Canada--Maps for children. 2. Children's atlases. I. Smith, Lori Joy, 1973-, illustrator II. Title.

G1115.D43 2017   j912.71   C2016-906100-0

Library of Congress Control Number: 2016956084

The illustrations were created digitally with an iPencil in Procreate for iPad and finished in Photoshop.
The text is set in Blue Sheep and Jolly Good Proper.

Edited by: Maria Birmingham and Debbie Rogosin
Designed by: Diane Robertson

ONTARIO ARTS COUNCIL
CONSEIL DES ARTS DE L'ONTARIO
an Ontario government agency
un organisme du gouvernement de l'Ontario

Canada Council   Conseil des Arts
for the Arts   du Canada

Canada

Manufactured in Shenzhen, Guangdong, China, in January 2017, by WKT Co. Ltd.
Job #16A2788

A   B   C   D   E   F

Publisher of Chirp, chickaDEE and OWL
www.owlkidsbooks.com

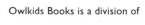 Owlkids Books is a division of  Bayard
CANADA